ARL Profiles:
Research Libraries 2010

William Gray Potter, University of Georgia

Colleen Cook, McGill University

Martha Kyrillidou, Association of Research Libraries

With Contributions from
Jennifer Rutner, Columbia University
Michael Maciel, Texas A&M University
David Green, Association of Research Libraries
Sarah Lippincott, Association of Research Libraries
Yolanda Glass, Association of Research Libraries
Nicholas Woolf, Woolf Consulting Inc.

April 2011
Association of Research Libraries

ARL Profiles: Research Libraries 2010

William Gray Potter, University of Georgia

Colleen Cook, McGill University

Martha Kyrillidou, Association of Research Libraries

With Contributions from
Jennifer Rutner, Columbia University
Michael Maciel, Texas A&M University
David Green, Association of Research Libraries
Sarah Lippincott, Association of Research Libraries
Yolanda Glass, Association of Research Libraries
Nicholas Woolf, Woolf Consulting Inc.

April 2011
Association of Research Libraries

ISBN 1-59407-863-7
EAN 9781594078637

Contents

Introduction

Research libraries are delivering value to their constituencies in many new ways and the traditional way of capturing their activities through annual statistics[1] does not adequately communicate in isolation the value and impact of these institutions on the life of their users. Research libraries are delivering value by becoming more closely engaged with the research, teaching and learning processes of their faculty, students and researchers within their institutions. Other recent studies also articulate this message eloquently and have been recently published both in the UK[2] and in the US.[3]

The current ARL report summarizes a multi-year effort that captures evidence in the form of narrative profiles as it delivers the message of the value and contributions of research libraries during transformative times. When ARL library directors were interviewed in 2005 and asked to describe a research library in the 21st century, there was general sentiment that the suite of ARL Statistics and the toolkit of services offered through the ARL Statistics and Assessment capability were insufficient in answering this question. There was a call for greater flexibility in describing today's research library in qualitative terms. Textual narrative descriptions of collections, services, collaborative relations, and other programs, as well as physical spaces were deemed necessary if the essence of a research library and the transformation of its collections and services are to be described and evaluated.

This report summarizes the themes and contributions that emerged from the narrative descriptions submitted by ARL libraries. The Statistics and Assessment Committee discussed these themes and considered how to use them to shape the committee's future work and accelerate ARL's Statistics and Assessment work as indicated in the 2010–2012 ARL Strategic Plan.

Contributing to the Common Good

Section I: Summary of Findings with Recommendations [4]

BACKGROUND

During 2007 and 2008, members of the ARL Statistics and Assessment Committee in collaboration with other ARL member leaders developed narrative descriptions of their libraries called profiles to capture the emerging transformations happening at their institutions. The end result was a small collection of model profiles, which offered an alternative way of describing research libraries in addition to the ARL Statistics.

In the spring of 2009, ARL invited all member libraries to submit profiles. At that time, the following plan detailed how the profiles were to be used:

- The narratives would stand on their own as accompanying descriptions to the quantitative annual statistical data.
- The profiles would be analyzed to identify possible new descriptive variables for the annual statistics that represent today's research library.
- All materials from the analysis would be made available to the ARL membership.

The long-term goal was to explore testing and development of a multi-factor index measuring and assessing collections, services, and collaborative relations using new data elements identified in the profiling process. Such an index would be an alternative to the ARL Library Investment Index, which is a summary measure of relative size among the university library members of the Association and serves as one indicator of potential for ARL membership.[5]

RLLF Fellows Analyze Themes in ARL Library Profiles

Four participants in the 2009-10 ARL Research Library Leadership Fellows (RLLF) program—Bob Fox (Georgia Tech), Pat Reakes (Florida), Brian Skib (Michigan), and Ann Snowman (Pennsylvania State)—selected the ARL member library profiles as the subject of their RLLF group project. The group worked with Martha Kyrillidou, Senior Director of ARL Statistics and Service Quality Programs, to develop the scope of their project, which was to review the profiles and make recommendations that might inform future changes to the ARL Annual and Supplementary Statistics.

The group drafted a list of themes from the profiles and gathered feedback from other RLLF fellows and colleagues in their libraries on the themes that warranted further study. The feedback included possible data-collection mechanisms and frequency. Some of the themes that emerged from this review of the profiles included: digital publishing, e-science/data curation and management, collaborations across all levels and on/off campus, assessment activities/space utilization, social networking tools/mobile applications, staffing changes, and collaborative collection building/development. The group's complete report and recommendations is available to the Task Force on Reviewing ARL Statistics, ARL Supplementary Statistics, and ARL Annual Salary Survey, which began work in October 2010. This task force is charged to review the three flagship ARL statistical publications and recommend data elements that should be dropped or revised.

Eighty-six ARL members submitted institutional profiles in time to be included in this analysis. ARL consultants and staff[6] used computer software, ATLAS.ti, to identify and analyze the ideas and themes contained in the narrative profiles. The software provided tools to isolate, code, and annotate the ideas and themes and to evaluate and rank them. The resulting set of reports not only broke each profile into a set of codes but also combined the codes into an overall view of the 86 responses, showing the frequency of themes and terms across all profiles as well as suggesting how libraries are similar and different.

It should be stressed that the profiles are not inventories or lists of every service or program that a library provides. Indeed, two libraries may host the same activity and one may discuss it at length in the profile while the other may not mention it at all. A profile reflects what a given library viewed as important at the time the profile was written. Therefore, when the frequency of an activity is mentioned below, bear in mind that it is the frequency of how many libraries mentioned that activity, not how many actually perform it.

Of the 86 libraries that provided profiles for analysis, 82 were academic libraries (7 Canadian, 22 US private, and 53 US public institutions). While all the profiles were valuable, this report focuses on the 82 academic libraries.

As an overview, six broad categories emerged from the analysis of the profiles. More detailed codes are grouped under each broad category and summarized in the second section of the report. Instead, major themes, similarities, and differences are discussed in this first section along with suggestions for codes that merit further investigation and discussion as possible new measures. The six categories discussed here are:

- Management and Self-Assessment
- Collaboration and Support—External
- Collaboration and Support—Internal
- Library Services
- Branch Libraries
- Collections

ANALYSIS OF SIX CATEGORIES

Management and Self-Assessment

Virtually all of the profiles mentioned the need for assessment as indicated in their discussion of specific tools, methods, and management strategies. Almost all reported some quantitative data when discussing management issues, but only 20% provided any qualitative measures. Interestingly, 25% did not mention collection size and 60% did not address the size of the user population. Over half mentioned building projects in the context of assessment activities.

One divergence of note is that public university libraries were more likely to discuss the parent university than private university libraries (85% vs. 59%) and that libraries ranked highest in the ARL Library Investment Index were less likely to mention the parent university (56% in the highest quintile of the index vs. 100% in the lowest quintile).

Themes that were widely reported included construction projects (55%), usage data (55%), the future of libraries (44%), and LibQUAL+® (45%).

Some themes that were mentioned infrequently were building-use statistics (13%), website analytics (10%), and assessing relevance of collections (13%).

Recommendation

Three common themes emerged that merit further discussion to define new measures or methods: developing mission and strategy statements, addressing collection development priorities, and providing the best way to describe the parent institution.

Collaboration and Support—External

All respondents addressed their collaborative relationships with other libraries and almost all provided a list of their partners. The most frequent activities of these collaborations were scholarly communication (65%), interlibrary loan (59%), and bibliographic enterprises (55%). Presumably, all ARL libraries are involved in interlibrary loan consortia, but not all reported them in their profiles.

The greatest divergence in this category was seen in the expression of a statewide mission, with 42% of public university libraries mentioning such a mission but only 5% of private university libraries noting one. Conversely, twice as many private university libraries mentioned holding a collection of national distinction as public university libraries, 64% vs. 30%. Interestingly, there was no similar distribution when members are broken down by the ARL Library Investment Index. In fact, libraries in the middle quintiles of the index tended to mention collections of national distinction more than libraries in the highest and lowest quintiles: 50% of the libraries in the second and third quintiles and 38% of the libraries in the fourth quintile mentioned such collections, while only 31% of the libraries in the first and fifth quintiles noted such collections.

Participation in a government depository program was mentioned in 29% of the profiles. Activities that were less frequently mentioned included shared storage (21%), working with museums (18%), and working with businesses (2%).

Recommendation

ARL should consider tracking collaborative efforts that are valued by ARL libraries, such as collaboration with non-library entities and shared storage facilities.

Collaboration and Support—Internal

Collaboration with other units within the parent university, usually departments or schools, were mentioned in 92% of the profiles. This collaboration was most often described as support for faculty success and student learning and took the form of faculty outreach and information literacy instruction.

Information literacy was mentioned more often by public university libraries (77%) than private university libraries (55%). Conversely, providing support for curriculum development was mentioned more often by private university libraries (64%) than public university libraries (45%). Promoting open access was more common in the top two quintiles of libraries in the ARL Investment Index (25%) than in the lower three quintiles (13%).

Other activities mentioned by at least a quarter of the libraries include technology support (51%), course management support (29%), and grant proposal support (25%). Less frequently mentioned are promoting open access (18%), leadership in copyright policy (10%), hosting electronic journals (9%), and marketing faculty research (4%).

Recommendation

A promising area for ARL assessment is the extent that member libraries are promoting open access.

Library Services

When mentioning specific library services in the profiles, the most common theme was providing innovative access to the library, notably in seeking expanded roles for the library. These included proactive orientation (89%), faculty outreach (61%), and a greater virtual presence (50%).

With regard to library services, there is little divergence among libraries by type and very little by funding, with a few exceptions. For example, laptop lending and extended hours were mentioned more often by libraries at the lower end of the ARL Investment Index while a service orientation was mentioned more frequently by the better-funded libraries. It is not possible to draw conclusions about these differences, but they might merit some examination.

Other common library services that were mentioned in the profiles include outreach to the community (44%), outreach services to students (38%), and small group workspaces (27%). Less frequently mentioned were resources available to the public (5%), services to alumni (4%), and wikis (2%).

Recommendation

This is perhaps the area where qualitative assessment is most needed. Measuring the effectiveness of services is difficult. LibQUAL+® has certainly helped, but additional methods of measuring the true benefit of services beyond usage statistics are needed.

Branch Libraries

Virtually all of the profiles discussed branch libraries, with special collections receiving the greatest attention (93%). Other branches commonly mentioned were information commons (66%), science and engineering (42%), health sciences (38%), law (30%), and art and architecture (28%). Less frequently mentioned were music/dance (23%), business (11%), and maps (9%). There is little divergence among libraries by type or by funding in this category.

Recommendation

Possible areas for increased measurement include the relative return on investment of branch libraries or, more generally, the distinctiveness of their value.

Collections

It is notable that the most common reference to collections in the profiles involves creating digital collections. This was mentioned by 96% of the libraries. A close second was preservation, mentioned by 85%. Digitizing was mentioned as a means of improving access by 88% of the libraries while 82% mentioned it as a preservation technique. There appears to be a greater emphasis on stewardship of the existing collections, either through digitization or preservation, rather than on building collections. Indeed, adding to collections was not overtly mentioned in any profile. Certainly, collection building is ongoing, but it was not prominent in the profiles.

Private university libraries were more likely to mention their nationally significant or distinctive collection than public university libraries (64% to 30%). Otherwise, there was little divergence by type or funding level.

Other themes mentioned by more than a quarter of the libraries included electronic theses and dissertations (37%), created digital objects (33%), government depository (29%), and microform collections (33%). Themes mentioned less frequently include map collections (9%), disaster recovery (4%), and weeding (4%). Electronic books were mentioned in 15% of the profiles.

Recommendation

The challenge of measuring the impact of the transition from print to digital has long been recognized within ARL. The profiles underline this challenge and should provide some guidance to the Statistics and Assessment Committee.

IN SUMMARY

The ARL Statistics and Assessment Committee completed the analysis of the profiles and has identified new directions as articulated in the above recommendations. When combined with other activities, notably the Lib-Value project[7] as well as local efforts to develop library scorecards, ARL hopes that the profiles can be used to refine existing programs as well as to identify new ones.

The profiles are a snapshot of the libraries at the time when these narratives were written. In many cases, the profiles are already obsolete. The committee considers that a strategy of systematic updating of the profiles once every four or five years may be a good option for the future as a complement to the numbers collected through the ARL Statistics survey, given the reporting burden and the resource demands of this activity. The analysis of the profiles has been a formative exercise that can help ARL articulate the transformations underway in member libraries and identify new metrics. Recognizing that these profiles and the analysis performed might be useful to others in the ARL community, the findings are made widely available. Indeed, it is hoped that this initial introduction whets your appetite for reading the lengthy analysis and materials provided by the libraries themselves as they articulate their efforts to remain relevant in an increasingly competitive environment.

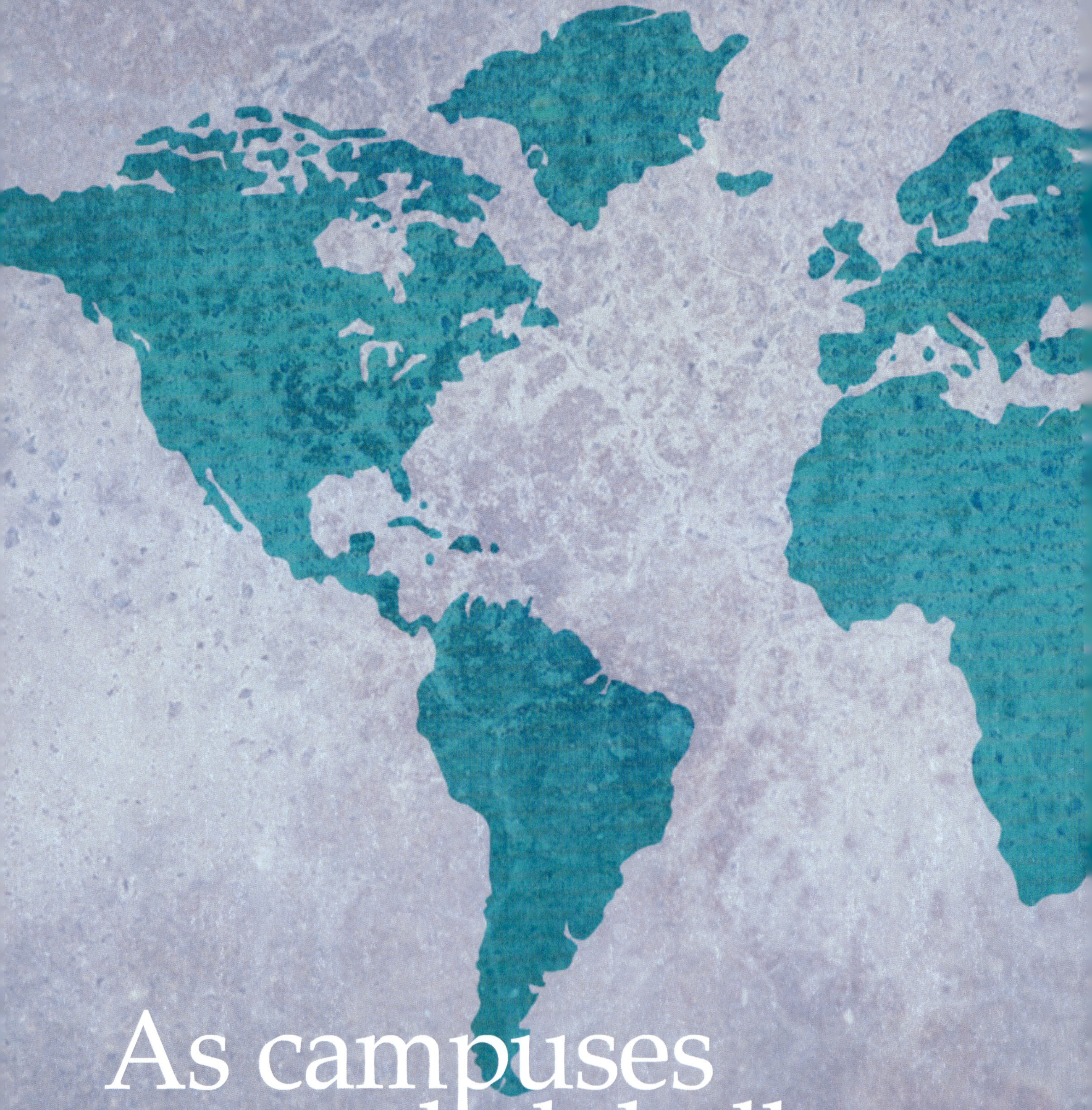

As campuses expand globally…

Section II: What do the profiles tell us?

The content analysis of the profile narratives are capturing important themes that are schematically described in the thematic analysis presented in Appendix A of this report. Four overarching meta-categories emerged addressing issues related to (1) management, (2) services, (3) collaborations, and (4) collections. The following section summarizes the themes from the content analysis of the profile narratives under these four general categories.

MANAGEMENT & ASSESSMENT

ARL members represent the leading research universities in the United States and Canada, as well as some of the nation's largest public libraries. Many member institutions are part of public university systems, others maintain branch campuses that serve different areas, and still others are private single-campus institutions. Some are classified by the Carnegie Foundation as research institutions with "very high research capacity." These libraries serve diverse populations of undergraduates, graduate students, faculty, and community members and promote the teaching and research missions of their institutions by making resources accessible and providing guidance on information and technology use.

Member libraries contain the largest and most diverse collections in North America. Most report collections of over 2 million print volumes, with many collections surpassing 5 million volumes. As part of formal and informal consortia and university systems, libraries provide access to even greater pools of information.

The holdings of member libraries include print materials, music scores and recordings, films, images, maps and increasingly significant collections of electronic resources. Most ARL libraries report tens of thousands of electronic journal subscriptions and access to hundreds of databases and electronic books. Each library also holds unique and rare materials as part of their special collections. These include rare books, manuscripts, archives, and important collections of audio and video recordings.

Vision

Libraries support the teaching, research, and public service missions of their institutions by acquiring, preserving, and providing access to information in all forms. The proliferation of electronic materials and the changing research needs and behaviors of faculty and students have brought about significant changes in library roles. To remain relevant and sustainable in this new environment, libraries have expanded and adapted their traditional activities. They increasingly concentrate on implementing user-based service models, developing digital infrastructure and tools to support information access, facilitating collaborative work, and providing instruction and guidance on information use.

Libraries strive to "be central to the University community's discovery, communication, and use of knowledge" (University of Colorado Libraries); "serve as a gateway and contributor to global networked information resources" (University of Connecticut Libraries); "symbolize and make real the concept of a university that reaches across departmental and disciplinary divisions" (Case Western University); become "a place—both physical and virtual—for the experimentation, production, and processing

> As campuses expand globally and students, faculty, and alumni become internationally mobile, libraries confront the need to offer resources not only across campus but around the world. While many libraries make their electronic resources available to the entire campus community, several also report a physical presence at overseas branch campuses.

of new knowledge" (Brown University); "lead the collaborative development of an academic information infrastructure that supports the changing needs of discovery, preservation, and transmission, as well as the application of knowledge, creativity, and critical thought" (Cornell); "help shape the creation of knowledge, conserve culture for posterity, and transform learning and research by providing preeminent services, collections and spaces" (Georgetown); provide "information, services and education in anyplace and at anytime" (University of New Mexico); "support the range of library user needs, from discovery and delivery to creation and sharing" (New York University); "inspire lifelong learning, advance knowledge, and strengthen our communities" (New York Public Library); "contribute to advancements in access to scholarly resources" (University of Oregon); "respect and defend user privacy and intellectual freedom" (SUNY Albany); and "connect users with resources that advance intellectual inquiry and discovery" (Texas A&M).

Libraries accomplish these diverse goals by developing innovative ways of organizing and preserving information; providing not only the materials, but the technology essential for research; offering guidance and expertise in information use; providing space for collaborative, interdisciplinary learning; preserving local and regional heritage and providing free library access to residents of their communities; building institutional repositories to house the university's research output; and continuing to collect and provide access to traditional library resources while evolving to meet the expanding needs of researchers.

As they consider the future, ARL libraries have identified collaboration, user-centered services, and digital infrastructure as key priorities to ensure the continued sustainability and relevance of academic libraries.

Collaboration among libraries will allow them to provide access to larger collections of resources, and make the most of limited funding for collection development (both print and digital). The University of British Columbia sees the "reenvisioning of the research library as globally networked entity, including changed ideas about what is locally 'collected.'"

Libraries will continue to make their services more user-centered, adapting to the continually changing needs to students, faculty, and the public. User-centered services include making information accessible where and when researchers need it, relying on frequent assessment to implement changes, repurposing library space to facilitate collaborative learning and provide media-rich study areas, improve collaboration with faculty and participation in instruction, and balance the need for accessibility with the mission of long-term preservation.

Libraries have already taken the lead in the development of the digital tools and infrastructure necessary to manage and preserve electronic resources, faculty research output, and scientific data. They see this becoming an even greater priority as they continue to migrate to electronic materials, expand their institutional repositories, and meet the challenge of bringing information to users wherever and whenever they want it. Providing convenient access to digital collections, including efficient searching and electronic document delivery, will also be key.

Libraries recognize that these efforts will need to be realized with limited resources and shrinking staff, and several libraries noted an emphasis on finding sustainable funding models and alternative sources of funds and the need for significant professional development and shifting roles.

Managing library and resources

Responding to limited resources and the changing needs of their users, many libraries are consolidating or reorganizing their services (including integrating library and information technology services) as well as expanding and reshaping the roles of librarians.

Libraries overwhelmingly report a shift in their role from "collections-based" to "service-based," and subsequent restructuring of departments and positions. At Northwestern University, three new departments were created to focus on user services, and the University of Maryland reports that its librarian and staff positions will "change dramatically and will be tied much more closely to users' assessed needs." Many others report the creation, reorganization, and merging of departments and positions to focus on strategic priorities like assessment, digital collection development, and diversity. They also report that librarian functions increasingly cross traditional departmental lines.

Several libraries report efforts to centralize collections, reduce their physical space, or consolidate purchasing between branches. The University of British Columbia Libraries reports that "the Library has moved from a highly distributed network of branches and service points to a more consolidated approach." Two of its libraries recently combined their reference and circulation desks. UCLA reports plans to "integrate the collections, services, and staff" of several of its numerous subject libraries into its larger libraries, and the University of Pittsburgh has seen several of its departmental libraries close over the past several years in response to the changing needs of its users. However, other member libraries continue to serve their institutions through decentralized systems of libraries, reference desks, and reading rooms spread across the campus.

Libraries are also redefining staff roles and identifying the skills sets necessary to fulfill the needs of future users and support the expanding array of library activities. The University of Alabama predicts the need for "profound structural reorganization and staff retraining to support the networked digital library." Brown University anticipates that its staff will shrink in the coming years, requiring librarians to develop greater expertise and more varied competencies. Many libraries report programs and partnerships designed to support professional development among their staff, including fellowship programs for post-graduates, regular forums and workshops, and job sharing programs. Librarians at many institutions pursue doctoral or additional Masters' degrees.

Though budget cuts have forced many libraries to respond to new demands by redefining the roles of their current staff, libraries report the creation of new positions in several key areas. These new positions were largely in the areas of technology, scholarly communications, and assessment. Other new positions include librarians or other staff dedicated to teaching and learning, international relations, outreach and marketing, intellectual property, data services, information literacy, and metadata.

Internship programs, many of which are grant-funded, benefit both the libraries and the interns, many of whom go on to pursue additional degrees or work in research libraries. Some internship programs are targeted to those who have already obtained an MLIS degree, while others focus on other graduate or undergraduate students with a demonstrated interest in research librarianship or working with primary source materials. Interns work on prototype projects, assist libraries in processing previously inaccessible materials, and support university archiving and the digitization of special collections. Some libraries also sponsor international librarian exchange programs that bring librarians from around the world to learn from and contribute to library activities.

Assessment and recognition

Responding to user needs and providing evidence of the continuing relevance of the library as a physical and virtual resource is vital to the sustainability of academic libraries. Assessment has become a strategic priority for many libraries as they compete for scarce resources and emphasize user-based service models.

Member libraries actively assess both quantitative (e.g. number of visits, volumes held) and qualitative (e.g. user satisfaction, behavior) data to help them better serve their populations and more effectively allocate resources. Assessment tools include environmental scans, feedback cards, faculty interviews and student advisory committees, collection of usage data, external reviews and surveys like LibQUAL+®[8] as well as software like Google Analytics. Some libraries, including SUNY Albany and Washington State University, report collecting data for all reference transactions, including the time of day and the type of question, in order to revise their services and hours.

New positions and job descriptions also support assessment activities. The University of Nebraska recently revised the position of an assistant dean to "include coordinating assessment efforts for the Libraries and to connect the Libraries efforts with campus assessment efforts." At the University of Hawaii, "An assessment team has been formed to regularize assessment as an ongoing part of the evaluation and improvement of library services."

Libraries report heavy use of both print and digital resources, though the growth of digital use frequently outpaces physical visits. The University of Georgia Libraries report that "circulation of printed materials has been fairly steady while the use of electronic resources has surged." The University of Illinois at Urbana-Champaign Library noted that "electronic access to content remains the preferred means for many users," and at the University of Massachusetts Amherst Libraries, 85 percent of transactions (views or circulation of paper and digital materials) in one month of 2009 were views of electronic materials, while the remaining 15 percent were physical items checked out from the library. The success of the library and its programs are measured in part by usage data, and some libraries noted that they have been able to expand their digital resources in response to the rapidly growing demand.

At the same time, many libraries, pointing to steady rates of visitors, emphasize that the print collections and the library building remain central to campus life.

Though quantitative data provide valuable information, many libraries report that their assessment efforts focus increasingly on qualitative data, such as the impact of the collections on research production, and the uniqueness of collections. The University of Notre Dame, for example, predicts that its future assessment activities will concentrate on the library's "impact on learning, teaching, and research, on campus and around the globe" rather than on quantitative data alone.

While assessment programs aim to help libraries develop a comprehensive picture of user behavior and satisfaction, a few key areas of interest emerge in qualitative assessments. Libraries are concerned with user knowledge of library services, preferred means of communicating with reference librarians and accessing library resources, and expectations for physical library space (technology, furniture, collaborative work spaces). Libraries also note the importance of assessing collection relevance, which helps them inform funding and preservation decisions.

> As they build information commons and reorganize space, many libraries have placed their reference desks in closer proximity to students who are conducting research, making librarians more accessible to users.

Many libraries report implementing concrete changes as a result of surveys they have conducted. For example, libraries report purchasing new technology and more comfortable seating, redesigning the library website, repurposing library space, extending hours, and adding or modifying services, in response to input from user surveys.

Development activities

ARL libraries are funded through a variety of sources including student fees, state funding, endowments, grants, and private philanthropy. Budget cuts due to the current economic environment have affected many institutions, requiring them to cut services and staff, reduce collection development budgets, and find creative ways to make the most of their limited resources. Particularly libraries at state-funded institutions report seeking out alternative sources of funding and intensifying their development initiatives.

Many ARL libraries seek grants (NEH, IMLS, etc.) and donations for diverse needs such as collection development, digitization and preservation, building and renovation, and creation of new programs. Fundraising programs in many libraries are fairly new, but have become increasingly important as libraries work with tightening budgets. The University of Illinois at Chicago Library, for example, report that "the Library is increasingly looking to private philanthropy to support and subsidize its efforts and growing unrestricted funds to address needs and fill gaps." Some libraries work with Friends of the Library groups on fundraising efforts, as well as on event coordination, promotion of collections and services, and community outreach.

SERVICES

Library facilities

The University of Maryland Libraries writes, "Space is becoming the new frontier." As print collections continue to grow and library space is repurposed to suit new workflows, libraries must develop solutions that balance collection development, ease of access, and cost-effectiveness. There is a growing need at many institutions for high-density, off-site storage for lesser used materials. Some libraries report that they already store some collections remotely, while others have plans in progress. These materials are delivered to patrons on demand, often within a day of the request. A few libraries report that they had faced initial skepticism about moving materials off-site, but that the ease of locating these materials in the library catalog, and their efficient delivery to campus had allayed many of these concerns. Some libraries are working to weed and discard redundant paper materials, or (in the case of microform) withdraw physical copies where digital versions exist.

While high-density storage alleviates strain on physical space, at least one library comments on the benefits of an open stack organization. The University of Chicago Libraries notes that "locating the Library's collection in open stacks at six on campus locations allows users to access all holdings rapidly and to make serendipitous discoveries while browsing."

In keeping with their mission of preserving culture and scholarship, ARL member libraries hold large collections of rare, primary source materials, from Civil War diaries to medieval manuscripts, in a variety of formats (images, documents, audio and video recordings, maps, etc.). Some of these collections include materials that are unique to the collection. Many libraries build special collections in areas relating to their regional history and culture, including personal papers, maps, government documents, and other materials. Libraries strive to build collections in their areas of expertise that are both broad and deep and may contain the largest collections of information in a given field.

The role of special collections is not just to preserve materials, but to make them available to students, faculty, and other researchers.

As Brown University Libraries writes, "These unique and extraordinary materials are not locked away as treasures in the attic, but are integrated fully into the ... teaching and learning experiences." By maintaining and building their special collections, libraries provide the academic community with the primary source materials necessary for scholarship. Digitization of these important archives is already taking place in many libraries and has been identified as a key priority by others. Some libraries actively promote their special collections with exhibits, digitization projects, and collaborations with university presses to publish books highlighting their holdings. Several libraries have constructed separate facilities for their special collections.

Special collections often house the University archives as well. University archives document the history of the institution (through photographs, documents, multimedia, biographic information, dissertations, etc.), and may also contain they personal materials of key figures from the institution. They also provide records management services for the institution.

In addition to special collections, ARL member libraries frequently include branch or subject libraries that serve different campus populations.

Science, math, and engineering libraries support undergraduate, graduate, and faculty research. They are frequently full-service branches with reference support, study areas, etc.

Health sciences libraries "use education, science, and technology to improve health," notes the University of Rochester. These libraries are frequently affiliated with a university hospital and may be housed on-site. Librarians may interact with faculty and students on campus, as well as with researchers and health care professionals at the hospital. Emory University's Woodruff Health Sciences Center Library, for example, has sponsored seminars and trainings, and has created online tutorials for faculty and students, as well as the staff of its affiliated hospital and clinics. At the University of Kentucky, librarians may accompany doctors on their rounds.

Many ARL health sciences libraries serve as regional libraries, and are part of the National Library of Medicine's National Network. They are frequently administered independently from other institutional libraries. Due to the nature of their collections, many of these libraries engage in local outreach, and provide healthcare information to unaffiliated members of the community. In addition to providing the latest medical research, they may also contain special collections and rare materials related to the history of medicine.

Law libraries are also frequently administered independently. They contain specialized collections in a range of subjects, from intellectual property law to health law. Some also offer specialized instruction in legal research.

Fine arts and architecture may be integrated into the main library, or occupy their own spaces. Art libraries have a diverse range of specialties, from illuminated manuscripts to the history of video games. Some have developed digital art archives from their collections. At least one member institution has an art library housed within a university-affiliated art museum.

Music libraries collect scores, recordings, music reference books, videos, and other materials that support faculty and student research. Some house special collections of rare primary source materials and specialized collections ranging from the history of jazz to materials relating to the seminal composer John Cage. At least one music library at an ARL institution has launched an effort to digitize some of its holdings.

Business, management, and economics libraries, like the William H. White Business Library at the University of Colorado, offer "study and research materials for management and administration, accounting, advertising, banking, finance, small business and entrepreneurship, marketing, real estate and transportation." Business librarians also offer instruction and research assistance to faculty and students.

Several ARL libraries include map libraries or geographic information centers that collect atlases, large and small scale maps, aerial photographs, and geographic reference materials. Some also support Geographic Information Systems (GIS).

As campuses expand globally and students, faculty, and alumni become internationally mobile, libraries confront the need to offer resources not only across campus but around the world. While many libraries make their electronic resources available to the entire campus community, several also report a physical presence at overseas branch campuses.

Instructional and group working spaces

The library building is increasingly used for instruction, collaborative learning, and technology use, creating a need for space that is adaptable, media-rich, and comfortable. Libraries report designing, renovating and refurnishing their buildings with flexible space in mind in order to meet diverse, continuously changing user needs. These spaces support multiple needs and learning styles (quiet spaces, group study rooms, multimedia classrooms, etc.).

Group work and study spaces allow graduate

The library building is increasingly used for instruction, collaborative learning, and technology use, creating a need for space that is adaptable, media-rich, and comfortable.

and undergraduate students to work collaboratively in close proximity to library resources and may include multimedia capabilities including Smart Boards and video conferencing technology.

Classrooms (both traditional and multimedia) and labs in the library building respond to the growing demand for instruction services and are used by library staff for information literacy and other instruction, and in some cases are open to use by faculty and graduate students.

The information commons has become the heart of many library buildings. These spaces offer a one-stop location for technology (desktop workstations, laptop lending, scanning and printing stations, cutting-edge software) and assistance (reference and technology support desks) to support collaborative learning and research. Often designed with undergraduate populations in mind, they may include vending machines with frequently needed supplies, seating that facilitates group work, and on-site tutoring. Information commons are often developed in partnership with information technology offices, providing the technology and reference support that students need in one place. Some libraries report that the establishment of information commons has led to an increase in library visits and have become the library's most heavily used resource.

Despite the expanding range of activities taking place in the library building, it remains important as a place for quiet study. The University of South Carolina Libraries, for example, report that quiet study areas were in high demand among its users. ARL Libraries frequently offer designated quiet study areas and provide private carrels for graduate students.

Customer-oriented services and expanded roles

As the University of Washington Libraries noted, "To realize the promise of the 21st century academic research library, it is essential that we continue to focus on our users and align our programs to better meet their needs." As they respond to changing workflows and expectations, ARL libraries increasingly emphasize service, convenience, and user satisfaction.

Libraries must respond to a demanding list of user priorities. Penn State Libraries report, "Students tell us that they want the Libraries to be welcoming and comfortable, that they want them to be technologically rich, and that everything must be fast, easy, and convenient."

Frequent assessment of services through institutional and external surveys, suggestion boxes, and meetings with student and faculty advisory committees helps libraries keep up with user priorities and identify key areas for improvement. Many libraries noted that they consistently see very high levels of user satisfaction and increased use of the library building, especially as they implement changes.

A comfortable, vibrant environment encourages learning and fosters community among library users. Libraries strive to engage with the campus community by bringing users into the library for a variety of activities including readings and film screenings and create a welcoming environment in a variety of ways, from providing comfortable furniture to offering personalized service. Some libraries have added cafés to allow users to refuel in the library and provide space for conversations and meetings. Iowa State University Libraries attributes an increase in library visits in part to the addition of its Bookends Café. Despite budget constraints, libraries have also identified expanded building hours as a priority.

Along with changes in physical space, libraries offer a growing number of virtual and outreach services that take resources to their users. These services are discussed in detail below.

Information delivery and traditional services

Reference support, document delivery (physical and electronic), and access to computers, remain essential library services, though libraries have developed innovative ways of delivering them. The University of British Columbia notes that, "increasingly the Library aims to take services beyond our buildings to where users are." This has meant the expansion of virtual reference services, improved document delivery, and increasing numbers of embedded and mobile librarians.

Reference services are no longer limited to in-person requests at the reference desk. The University of California Santa Barbara reports, "Recognizing that today's student and faculty no longer need to frequent the Library in person to access resources, the UCSB Library has made a concerted effort to expand our services beyond the Library." Libraries offer a broad array of convenient, user-centered reference services, including assistance by telephone, e-mail, chat, and text message. Libraries frequently report that virtual reference services are available 24 hours, sometimes through participation in a consortium, and one library reports that nearly 20 percent of its reference transactions are now virtual.

As they build information commons and reorganize space, many libraries have placed their reference desks in closer proximity to students who are conducting research, making librarians more accessible to users. At least one institution has implemented a program that allows patrons to page a staff member to their particular computer.

Many libraries report that overall reference transactions have declined, and a few, like Purdue University Libraries, reports that they have made an effort to "eliminate the traditional reference service." At these institutions, trained staff and graduate students provide assistance at service desks, while professional librarians are available for on-demand, in-depth support.

Embedded, subject, and mobile librarians serve as liaisons to specific disciplines, providing reference support, collection development services, course-specific instruction, and other assistance, often on-location. They may hold office hours or be housed within a department, develop subject guides, and provide course-specific instruction. Some ARL libraries offer subject librarians for every academic department on campus, and at least one institution reports providing subject-specific reference to researchers around the world in one of the library's areas of expertise.

Document delivery across campus, over the web, and between institutions supports the research needs of faculty and students, and allows libraries to share collections, store lesser used materials off-site, and provide access to materials for distance education students. Libraries offer paging services to make books available for pick up at the circulation desk, book delivery between campus libraries to allow users to pick up materials at the most convenient location, and US mail delivery for students located off-campus. Document delivery is increasingly virtual, and libraries frequently provide faculty and graduate students with on-demand scanning of articles and book chapters delivered directly to their e-mail accounts. At some libraries users can request delivery of materials directly through the online catalog.

Development and innovative use of technology

To support access to information, libraries are developing new search tools; utilizing innovative cataloging software; and creating interfaces that allow users to search various locally held collections, licensed content, and digital archives simultaneously. They are providing users with 24-hour access to content through their websites, creating customizable homepages that allow individual users to select the services and resources that are most important to them, and providing electronic delivery of information to desktops and mobile devices. Libraries are collaborating with other institutions and companies like Google to provide unprecedented access to digital materials through collective electronic archives, and are continuing to envision and develop innovative ways of accessing information. As Brown University Libraries writes, "New services (launched in the last five years) are designed to lessen the physical and intellectual barriers to knowledge and offer users the means to become more efficient and self-sufficient in their research."

The library website serves as the virtual gateway to the library's resources. Like many institutions, the Iowa State University Libraries has focused on making its website "more flexible, more user focused, more interactive, and more discovery oriented." Libraries have accomplished this by including prominently displayed search engines, building customizable homepages that provide convenient access to a user's most frequently consulted resources, and integrating with course management systems. Several libraries report that they have migrated their websites to the open-source content management system Drupal to facilitate rapid updating and simple navigation. Integrated or federated search interfaces, which allow library users to simultaneously search multiple catalogs or databases (within and among libraries), have become a staple of library websites. Libraries use a variety of software (either locally or externally developed) to facilitate federated search, including WebFeat, WorldCat Local, MetaLib, AquaBrowser, and PRIMO.

The capabilities of the library website may continue to expand in the future. Georgetown University, for example, aims to use the library website "as a vehicle to push reference and instructional services into a digital framework for virtual research, teaching and learning."

Social networking sites like Facebook, Twitter, as well as instant and text messaging provide librarians with new options for outreach to students, as well as for marketing library services. Libraries frequently offer reference services through chat and text messages, and provide information about the library through Facebook and Twitter. Some have also created blogs, wikis, Second Life environments, Flickr accounts, and RSS feeds, and have uploaded content to iTunesU and YouTube. Libraries are continuing to explore best practices in using social networking to engage with users and facilitate access to information.

To further the goal of providing constant access to information, many libraries report that their buildings offer comprehensive or extensive wireless access and some report that wireless Internet is available across the entire campus. Wireless access also supports laptop lending programs and reduces demand on networked workstations.

Libraries actively participate in creating the digital tools and infrastructure necessary to house and locate information. This includes developing and modifying open-source software for a variety of projects, including building digital archives (Cocoon, Solr, and Cooliris) and institutional repositories (Fedora), supporting digital humanities research (the bibliographic manager Zotero), managing course reserves (ReservesDirect, developed by Emory University), improving electronic catalogs (the eXtensible Catalog Project), managing their websites (Drupal), and improving the capabilities of integrated library systems (Open Library Environment project).

Some libraries use wikis for internal collaboration. Georgetown University Libraries uses a wiki application to "facilitate collaboration between staff who often work on related goals and objectives, and to make it easier for staff to engage, share and learn about library wide projects." The University of Georgia Libraries developed a wiki to interact with library users.

COLLABORATION & SUPPORT

Internal collaboration

As a center for research and learning, libraries collaborate every day with faculty, students, academic departments, and information technology offices. Libraries facilitate interdisciplinary work by sponsoring digitization projects that span several academic areas, providing learning and research commons where students and faculty from all areas are encouraged to engage with each other, and by collaborating with faculty on research. They bring the campus community together by holding lectures, exhibits, and conferences, and other events. And they support faculty and students in an increasingly broad array of activities.

Supporting faculty success

In addition to traditional support services like reference assistance and collection development, faculty rely on the library for a wide variety of needs including data management, curriculum development, and archiving and marketing their research output.

Libraries develop innovative solutions for information access and bring library services to faculty where they work. Liaison librarians continue to work with faculty to determine their needs (in terms of collections and services) and provide reference support, but now they may do so as "embedded" librarians with on-location office hours. Libraries bring resources to faculty where and when they need them by offering free document delivery (physical and virtual) and by building robust electronic collections.

Support for faculty research does not end with reference. Libraries frequently assist in grant-writing activities, including identifying sources of funding. Libraries also collaborate with academic departments to fund fellowships and visiting scholars. Furthermore, libraries help their faculty promote their research by providing open access journals and institutional repositories, helping faculty deposit their articles in external digital repositories, and by sponsoring lecture series where faculty can share their research.

Faculty often see libraries as partners in the instruction and curriculum development process. Many libraries help design student learning outcomes, populate course web pages with relevant materials, integrate technology into assignments and teaching, build online courses and tutorials, help faculty build courses based around specific items or collections, and team-teach courses on information literacy and research methods.

Additionally, librarians are often involved in the development and implementation of course management systems, a tool that allows instructors to bring together readings, assignments, course reserves, and library resources in one course web page. As the University of California, Los Angeles Libraries notes, involving librarians in the implementation of its course management system "ensures the integration of relevant services and resources—for example, reserves, links to recommended resources, copyright information—into the system, where instructors can easily incorporate them into the pages for each course." In many cases, librarians also offer instruction and assistance to faculty, graduate students, and undergraduates in the effective use of course management systems.

Friends of the Library organizations and joint committees with faculty foster opportunities for dialogue and collaboration at many institutions. Workshops on issues such as open access publishing also serve to engage faculty in the library. At one institution, a planned Faculty Engagement department will focus exclusively on these efforts.

Supporting student learning and outcomes

As the University of Alabama Libraries writes, "the Libraries are in a very real sense both an academic component of the University and a support mechanism for students." Librarians play an integral role in information literacy instruction, provide reference and assistance in and outside the library building, and populate many course management systems and course websites. Libraries also offer study skills workshops, tutoring, lecture series, film nights, exhibits, and readings in the library building to engage with undergraduate populations.

From participating in freshman orientation to offering research and technology assistance for coursework, librarians take a variety of opportunities to promote library resources and services to students. Some exceptional outreach activities include offering awards for undergraduate research that makes outstanding use of the library's holdings; employing a "mobile librarian" who provides library services across campus; sponsoring a book collecting competition for undergraduates; providing reserve copies of particularly expensive, high-demand text books; and actively soliciting user suggestions. Libraries must increasingly reach out to undergraduates through the Web, and some report that they have developed sites that contain resources and tools specifically targeted to this population.

From the time students arrive on campus, libraries begin promoting their resources and services. Libraries often participate in freshman orientation, introducing incoming students and their parents to the library's resources. Rather than providing a general orientation session for incoming students, some libraries encourage on-demand instruction geared toward a particular course. Some libraries even offer for-credit courses in information literacy or research methods.

Libraries are increasingly called upon to provide instruction in information literacy, and frequently help incorporate library research instruction into required undergraduate courses. They also offer seminars on software and technology use, advanced workshops for graduate students, and access to electronic research guides and tutorials. Several libraries report that they have labs in the library building dedicated to instruction, and the University of Georgia Libraries, for example, reports that its reference librarians increasingly concentrate on instruction. Libraries have developed a variety of collaborations and services to respond to the demand, including general undergraduate education; advanced information management workshops or for-credit courses; one-on-one research assistance, information literacy assessment; and creation of subject guides and course web pages that help students access relevant, reliable materials.

Information literacy instruction helps students become better researchers, and also exposes them to the breadth and depth of library collections, and many institutions have identified it as a key student learning outcome, particularly in relation to online resources. The level of instruction offered varies between institutions. Many libraries report that information literacy instruction has been integrated into required freshman composition courses. Some institutions even require that these courses include a library research session. Other libraries provide these services on request to instructors and students. Some libraries offer for-credit courses in information literacy or research methods and the University of Arizona libraries have been asked to create a minor in online information use.

Learning and information commons have become particularly effective outreach tools by bringing in students and putting them in close proximity to librarians who can assist them with assignments and providing them with the technology and equipment they need for their research and assignments.

Students increasingly need and expect access to computers in the library. Libraries aim to provide students with the latest technology, as well as the support they need to use it effectively. The information commons often hosts the library's highest concentration of computers, putting students in close proximity to reference

Learning and information commons have become particularly effective outreach tools by bringing in students and putting them in close proximity to librarians who can assist them with assignments and providing them with the technology and equipment they need for their research and assignments.

and technology support. Many libraries provide hundreds of desktop workstations, and at some institutions, the library is the largest computer lab on campus. These computers are often equipped with multimedia software for web design, graphic design, and audio and video production, among others. Specialized and subject libraries may provide their students with discipline-specific software.

In addition to desktop computers, libraries offer a variety of equipment for use in the building and for loan. Students often have access to loaner laptops that allow students to work throughout the library and across campus, as well as digital video cameras, still cameras, media viewing stations, printers, and scanners. Providing users with this equipment in the library building allows librarians to offer convenient technology support and assistance. Some libraries have digital media labs, or programs dedicated to helping students and faculty use library equipment to incorporate media into their courses and assignments. Some libraries (Brown University Libraries) also offer "support for classroom media technology as well as the digital video recording of classroom lectures and campus events."

Collaboration with departments and schools

Libraries participate in a variety of productive collaborations with information technology departments at their institutions to support and improve library technology. Information technology departments are often involved in the creation of information commons, as well as in developing course management systems; providing information literacy instruction; establishing methods for data curation; advancing scholarly communications initiatives; jointly staffing multimedia labs; developing institutional repositories; developing software for cataloging, searching, and managing the website; and exploring cloud computing, computational research, and digital library initiatives. At some institutions, information technology departments manage library servers.

Events such as lectures, readings, book clubs, film screenings, conferences, and exhibits bring the community into the library building and reflect the library's commitment to engaging in campus life. Libraries collaborate with academic departments, campus bookstores, alumni, student groups, and other libraries to offer a variety of activities in the library and across campus.

External collaborations

External collaborations include partnering with businesses, service providers, organizations, research and bibliographic enterprises, governments, museums, and other libraries to improve technology, pool resources, provide access to information, preserve collections, and advance the field of library science.

Libraries work with service providers to improve technology, advance digitization projects, and support open access; develop software that serves their institutional needs (Dartmouth built its Journal Usage Reports product with Thomson ISI Web of Knowledge); and increase the research capacity of bibliographic software (Emory University collaborated with Zotero to improve its digital humanities research capabilities). Several libraries participate in the extensible Catalog Project (XC) that will provide libraries with new ways of making their collections searchable.

Collaborations with research and bibliographic enterprises support improved cataloging, preservation of digital content, and dissemination of research materials. ARL libraries have collaborated on the development and population of repository projects such as the HathiTrust and Portico.

Many libraries are members of OCLC, including some founding members. Beyond holding membership in the network, some libraries collaborate with OCLC to improve their institutional electronic catalogs, including implementing WorldCat Local. Many ARL libraries use OCLC software such as ILLiad and ContentDM, and assessment tools like OCLC Collection Analysis, and submit their cataloguing information for inclusion in WorldCat.

Libraries collaborate with museums (on and off-campus) on projects such as digital preservation of local history, facilitating online access to museum holdings, and sponsoring and participating in exhibits. Some libraries also report partnerships with local museums that provide students with access to museum collections.

Collaborations with businesses include digital preservation projects, agreements with commercial publishers to support open access publishing, partnerships with Amazon.com to make resources available on-demand, and participation in the Google Books project. Some more unique collaborations with businesses include Texas Tech's collaboration with Pixar, Microsoft, and Cray on 3-D animation research, and collaborations between the Utah Ski Archive at the University of Utah and local winter recreation businesses.

The Google Books project is based on the involvement of several ARL libraries. In one case, a consortium of universities, the Committee on Institutional Cooperation, collectively agreed to digitize their collections in partnership with Google. Libraries collaborate with Google in order to make their holdings widely accessible as well as to ensure their preservation.

Collaborations with other libraries

Collaboration between libraries supports a wide range of activities including digitization projects, software development, collection development, and providing workshops and conferences.

Libraries rely on traditional Interlibrary Loan programs as well as supplementary borrowing agreements and consortia, like Borrow Direct, to provide their users with timely, cost-effective access to resources. Like many others, the University of Arizona Libraries report that they "have moved away from a model of 'just in case' collection development to a strategy of 'just in time' delivery." To expedite turnaround time, libraries increasingly deliver electronic resources and have implemented unmediated delivery services for electronic articles.

To make the most of limited space and funding, libraries at both public and private institutions use shared off-site storage facilities and developing collections in cooperation with other universities in their region. Access to materials in shared collections is often facilitated by electronic document delivery. Examples include the University of Maryland's collaboration with Johns Hopkins University, and RECAP, a partnership between Columbia University, Princeton University, and the New York Public Library.

Many member libraries participate in formalized consortia, such as the Five College Libraries (University of Massachusetts) and the Committee on Institutional Cooperation in the Midwest, , and others are part of university systems. Libraries also participate in eScholarship projects such as the HathiTrust and Google Books to share their resources with an even broader audience.

Digitization projects provide ample opportunities for collaboration as libraries work with other institutions, associations, museums, and state and local governments to collect, digitize, and archive photographs, documents, books, and other materials.

Contributing to the common good

Libraries support not only the teaching and research missions, but the public service missions of their institutions. To this end, they provide outreach services to the community, archive nationally or regionally significant collections, contribute to the latest developments in the field of library science, lead efforts to promote open access and raise awareness of scholarly communications issues, and in some cases serving as research libraries for entire university systems. Some member libraries are part of land-grant institutions or state university systems, and as such are required to serve both the academic community and the public.

Libraries house diverse collections of primary source materials that are valuable not only for scholars on campus, but often for the local community and for visiting researchers from around the world. Many libraries collect geographically relevant materials and archive the personal papers of prominent historical figures. Some state institutions, such as the University of Kentucky, work with other libraries around the state to gather materials related to regional history. As official government depositories, many ARL members collect documents, maps, patents and other materials from federal and state governments, the United Nations, and the European Union, in both print and digital form.

Contributing to the cultural, intellectual, and economic development of their communities is central to the mission of research libraries.

By establishing partnerships with public schools, archiving public records and regional history, and providing the public with free access to resources, ARL libraries benefit their local communities. Many libraries have programs on and off campus to promote community involvement. These include, for example, establishing a family history project at a subject library, providing research support for small businesses, presenting lecture series and exhibits that are open to the public, building digital collections that can be accessed off-site, and teaching free classes on information literacy and computer skills. Some libraries work with local partners to provide the community with information on health, diversity, and other issues.

Whether working with K-12 to integrate technology into the classroom, offering lectures and exhibitions that are open to the public, or making online resources available to alumni, libraries support lifelong learning. Research librarians often serve as teachers on campus (providing assistance and teaching research skills to students) and off (bringing information literacy and technology education to public libraries and schools in the community). Lecture series and readings hosted in the library encourage members of the community to engage in academic life.

Librarians engage with their professional communities by writing for and editing scholarly journals; presenting at conferences; serving on working groups, committees, and editorial boards; and producing other work that advances thought in the field of library and information science. In some cases, librarians are required by their institutions to make contributions to research as part of the professional reward systems. Librarians also participate in a variety of professional associations, teach courses in library science programs, and host professional development and training on their own campuses. They also work to set standards and explore best practices with national and international visibility. The University of Chicago Libraries reports that its University Librarian is participating in the Working Group on Bibliographic Control to advise the Library of Congress on the implications of new technology for bibliographic practices.

Librarians also take part in a variety of service programs in their communities and around the world. Cornell University's Law Library, for example, is currently working on providing free online access to legal resources in Liberia. With the help of external grants, the University of Illinois at Urbana-Champaign Libraries has provided support to professional development programs in countries such as Costa Rica, Nigeria, and Vietnam. The University of Louisville Libraries employs two Outreach Librarians who work with the city on key issues like diversity and healthcare.

Expanding access to the institution's research output is central to the mission of research libraries, and many actively take part in scholarly communications activities on their campuses, particularly through developing and hosting digital repositories, and raising awareness of scholarly communications issues. Some libraries have established copyright or intellectual property offices to provide guidance to the academic community on scholarly communication issues. Others sponsor workshops, make librarians available for consultations about scholarly communication issues, and develop online tutorials about authors' rights. Several have a dedicated scholarly communications librarian. A few member libraries have relationships with their university presses that open up new opportunities for scholarly communications activities, including publishing open-access journals.

By formally endorsing open access, building infrastructure, providing open access content, and exploring best practices, libraries have taken the lead in promoting the concept of open access. The University of Kansas became the first public university in the United States to adopt a formal open access policy, and other ARL members have passed similar resolutions. Many libraries provide assistance and expertise to faculty interested in open access publishing and host their own open access journals.

COLLECTIONS

Collection development priorities

Collection development responds to the current and future needs of faculty, graduate students and undergraduates. As libraries cope with limited financial resources, dedicate more library space to collaborative learning and technology, and respond to the evolving needs and expectations of their users, electronic materials have become major areas of collection growth. Several libraries report that more than half of their collection budget supports the acquisition of electronic resources.

Migrating from print to digital collections, using limited budgets most efficiently, and eliminating duplicate resources within libraries and library systems have become top priorities. Libraries must balance their missions of bringing high-quality resources to their students and faculties, with limited financial and physical resources. The University of Maryland reports that its collection development policy specifies that "some print collections will greatly reduce over time and library space will be repurposed to serve a variety of user needs."

Libraries that belong to consortia or university systems benefit from collective purchasing power that allows to them to provide the resources their students need despite limited budgets and the high cost of electronic journals and other materials. Washington State University said, "Collaboration with other institutions, always important to the WSU Libraries, is becoming more critical as costs increase and local resources are increasingly strained."

Libraries also noted that digitizing and providing access to electronic resources for their entire communities was a high priority. Penn State Libraries report, "Being geographically dispersed as we are, our collection development is guided by the principle that no matter which campus students attend, nor where faculty members reside, they should have equitable access to all library resources."

Stewardship

The University of Michigan Libraries writes, "The role of libraries has always been to collect and preserve objects of scholarly importance over the long term, and we take that responsibility just as seriously today as we did before the start of the digital era." Libraries are constantly developing new strategies to ensure the long-term preservation of their institutions' physical and digital collections.

Archiving and cataloging materials to make them accessible and easy to find is a constant process. Librarians work to catalog newly acquired collections as well as holdings that have been "hidden" or inaccessible in the past.

Preservation departments or labs are responsible for both the maintenance of the library's general collections, and the repair and conservation of rare and fragile materials. Conservators may have additional expertise (disaster recovery) or responsibilities (overseeing the digitization of fragile materials) as needed. Some libraries have active disaster preparedness plans to protect their collections in the event of an emergency, and library conservators may be trained in disaster recovery.

Digitization not only provides access to a library's holdings, but ensures their long-term preservation (particularly in the case of rare, damaged, or fragile documents). Libraries rely on both institutional archives and organizations like Portico, the HathiTrust, and the MetaArchive Cooperative to provide solutions for long-term preservation of digital materials. The longevity of digital archives themselves continues to be a concern. Developing strategies that make these archives physically and financially sustainable is a concern for many libraries.

Libraries have taken the lead in developing, maintaining, and populating institutional repositories, as part of their mission to preserve and promote the research output of the university and to support open access to scholarship. Institutional repositories house faculty and graduate student articles, theses and dissertations, and audiovisual materials, among other content, and make them freely available to the public online. Many libraries report great success in recruiting materials and support for institutional repository efforts.

In addition to creating local digital archives, libraries also report participating in collaborative digitization projects with regional partners, consortia, governments, repositories like the HathiTrust, and companies like Google. Collaborative projects pool the resources of each institution and support the development of comprehensive, standardized digital collections that provide free access to public domain information and long-term archival solutions for universities.

Digital collections

Digital collections include both external digital content (journals, databases, image collections, etc.), internal digital content (born-digital content and digitized materials from the library's collection), and collections of electronic journals and books.

Outside digital resources supplement the academic library's local electronic collections and provide users with important sources of data, primary source materials, and the latest research. Libraries hold subscriptions to a variety of outside digital resources that are often searchable on or off campus, 24 hours a day.

Collections of born-digital content center on the institutional repository, as discussed earlier. Institutional repositories house and provide access to all of the scholarly output of the campus community, much of it born-digital. To support access to the research output of the university, many institutional repositories also archive theses and dissertations. Digital collections may also include electronic journals hosted by the institution. Several libraries report efforts to capture and archive born-digital content. The University of California, Davis Libraries for example, has partnered with New York University Libraries and the University of North Texas Libraries to develop "Web archiving tools that will be used by libraries to capture, curate and preserve collections of Web-based government and political information."

Digitized content gives students, faculty, researchers, and the general public access to information when and where they need it, and therefore represents a significant method of reducing barriers to access. Because so many digitization projects involve special collections and unique holdings, these materials might otherwise have remained "hidden." Facilitating access to digital content involves more than scanning documents and populating archives. Libraries must provide metadata and create search tools that allow users to locate the documents they need, "develop contextual information and supplementary materials ... that enable users to have a richer understanding of the original materials" (Brown University Libraries), and build sustainable funding models that will allow these collections to remain permanently available.

Libraries actively digitize media in a variety of formats (video, audio, images, and text), and may provide digitization equipment for faculty and student use. They use various software to manage digitized collections, including CONTENTdm. Some collections are available to the public, while others are exclusively available to the campus community. Several libraries participate in inter-institutional projects to digitize documents, such as the National Endowment for the Humanities funded Library of Congress National Digital Newspaper Program.

As they digitize collections, libraries also develop metadata that allows researchers to locate the materials they need. Brigham Young University reports, "As the Library moves to a primarily digital environment, great care is taken in creating and providing quality metadata that will aid in the ongoing preservation of collections." Some libraries employ specialized metadata librarians, or provide professional development for staff in this area to ensure that digital collections are searchable within the university and through major bibliographic networks. At least one institution allows faculty and students to tag records to improve searching.

Despite high costs, libraries have built robust collections of electronic journals and e-books. Collection of e-books has generally been a later phenomenon compared to electronic journals. Libraries report disparate experiences in e-book collecting. One quarter of the books purchased by the University of Arizona in the 2008 – 2009 academic year were e-books. On the other hand, Case Western Reserve University Libraries reports that e-books "have not yet made significant inroads in the collection." Just a matter of time!

... set standards and explore best practices with national and international visibility.

Conclusion

The profile narratives are truly time bound and are probably somewhat obsolete already as research libraries are evolving and transforming their operations shifting from what may be symbolically described as a book-based print model to a digital-based electronic delivery of information. One of the main goals of capturing these roles that are libraries are engaged in through the qualitative profiles was to provide the descriptive evidence that demonstrate the contributions research libraries are making in a changing environment. In an environment where books and other information resources are rapidly becoming available in digital form research libraries are called upon to define the new metrics that will describe their enduring contributions and values in the 21st century. Research libraries are witnessing an era where their core symbolic information artifact, the printed page, is transformed, and it is difficult to predict what are the enduring metrics for the 21st century research library.

Yet we know from these profile narratives that the 21st century research library is a place where research, learning, knowledge and information exchange is in high demand, where users satisfy their information needs, and where professionals are providing high levels of service to support enduring access to information resources. The profiles are a testament to our responsibility to capture those valuable roles and articulate effectively the contributions libraries are making into the life of their users.

EndNotes

1 Association of Research Libraries. *ARL Statistics* (annual): www.arlstatistics.org.

2 Research Libraries UK (RLUK) and Research Information Network (RIN). "The Value of Libraries for Research and Researchers" (March 2011) http://www.rin.ac.uk/our-work/using-and-accessing-information-resources/value-libraries-research-and-researchers.

3 Megan Oakleaf, *The Value of Academic Libraries: A Comprehensive Research Review and Report*. Chicago: Association of College and Research Libraries, 2010.

4 A modified version of Section 1 was first published as: William Gray Potter, Colleen Cook, and Martha Kyrillidou. "ARL Profiles: Qualitative Descriptions of Research Libraries in the Early 21st Century." *Research Library Issues: A Bimonthly Report from ARL, CNI, and SPARC*, no. 271 (August 2010): 25–31, http://www.arl.org/resources/pubs/rli/archive/rli271.shtml.

5 ARL Index, http://www.arl.org/stats/index/.

6 A consultant, Nicholas Woolf, was retained to guide the use of ATLAS.ti and to prepare reports. Jennifer Rutner (Columbia University), Michael Maciel (Texas A&M University), David Green (ARL), and Martha Kyrillidou (ARL) coded the profiles in detail.

7 Regina Mays, Carol Tenopir, and Paula Kaufman, "Lib-Value: Measuring Value and Return on Investment of Academic Libraries," *Research Library Issues: A Bimonthly Report from ARL, CNI, and SPARC*, no. 271 (August 2010): 36–40, http://www.arl.org/resources/pubs/rli/archive/rli271.shtml.

8 For more information on the LibQUAL+® service, see: www.libqual.org; For the suite of tools offered by ARL under StatsQUAL®, see: www.statsqual.org.

Summary of Codes

This diagram represents a summary of the codes and supercodes developed during the analysis. See the Technical Notes for a description of the codes and supercodes in this diagram: http://www.arl.org/bm~doc/technical-notes.pdf

OVERVIEW

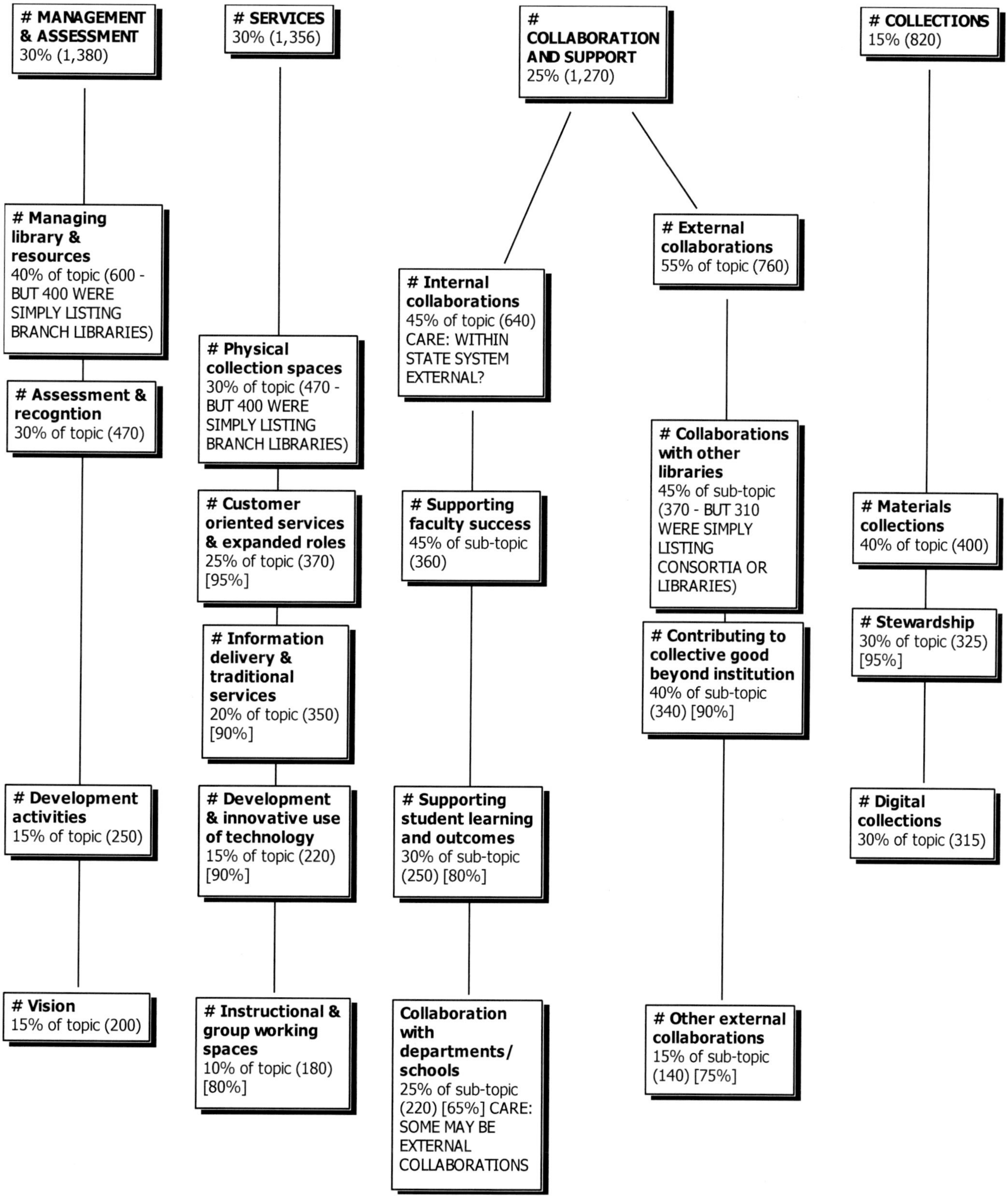

MANAGEMENT & SELF-ASSESSMENT

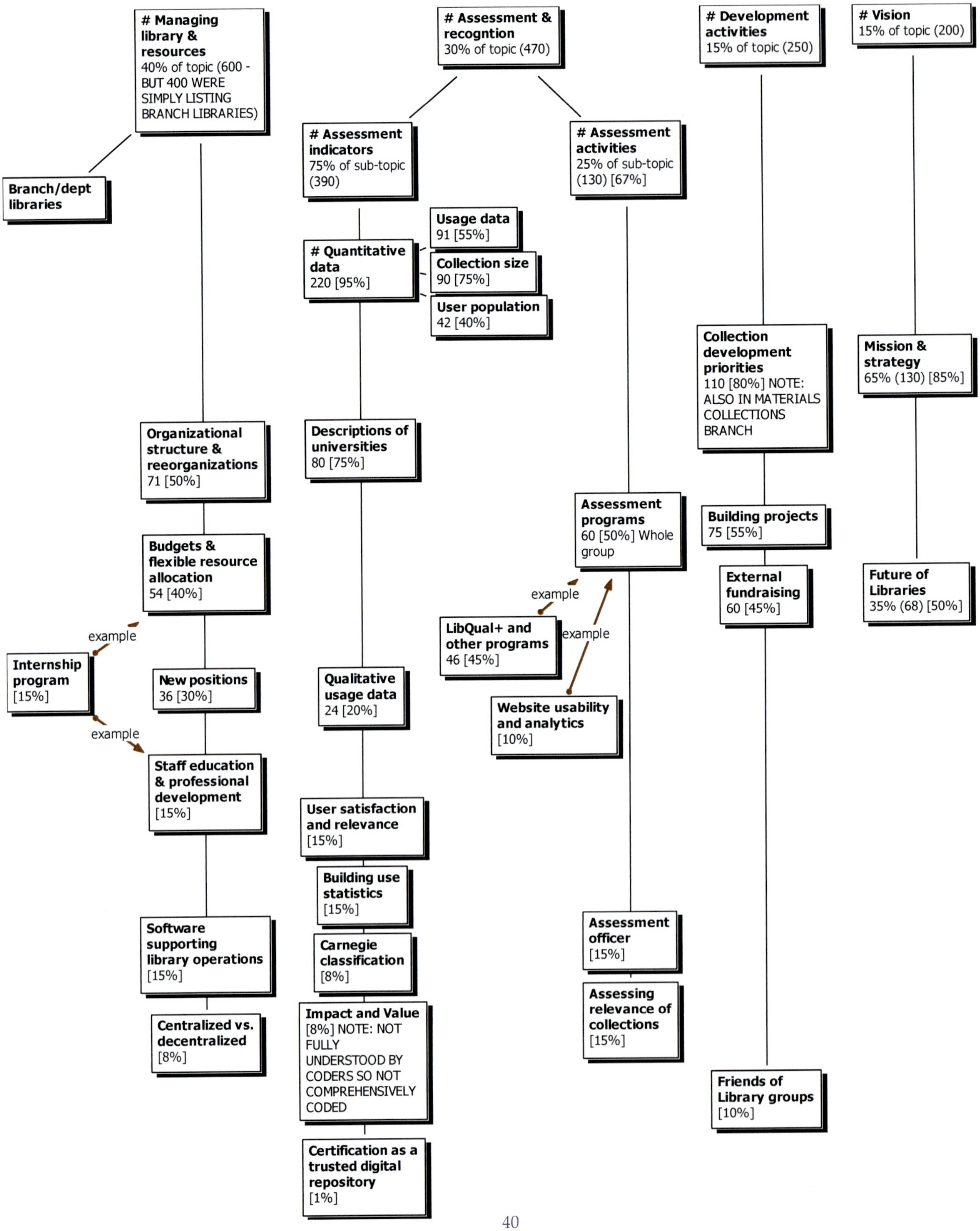

COLLABORATION & SUPPORT – EXTERNAL

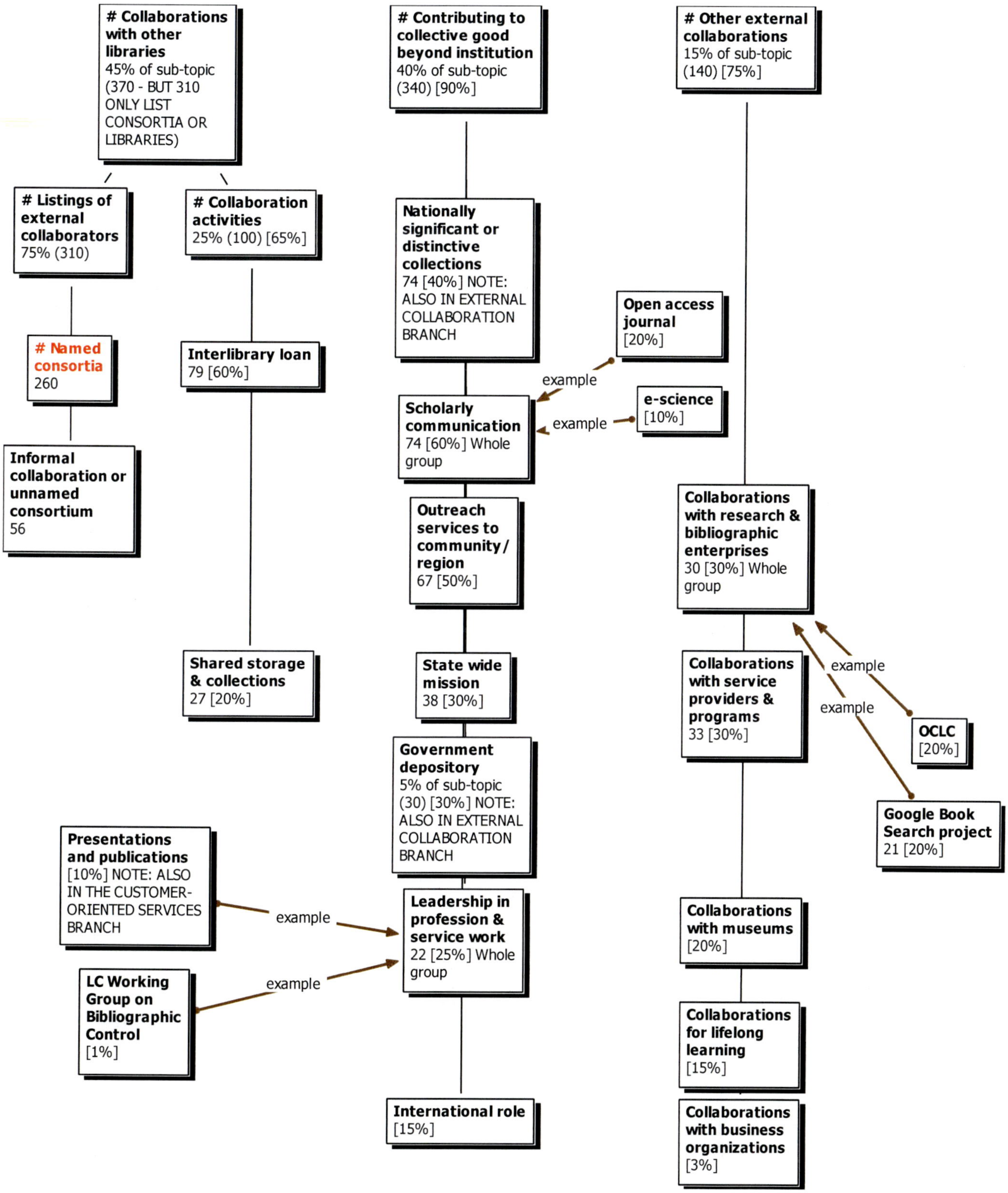

COLLABORATION & SUPPORT – INTERNAL

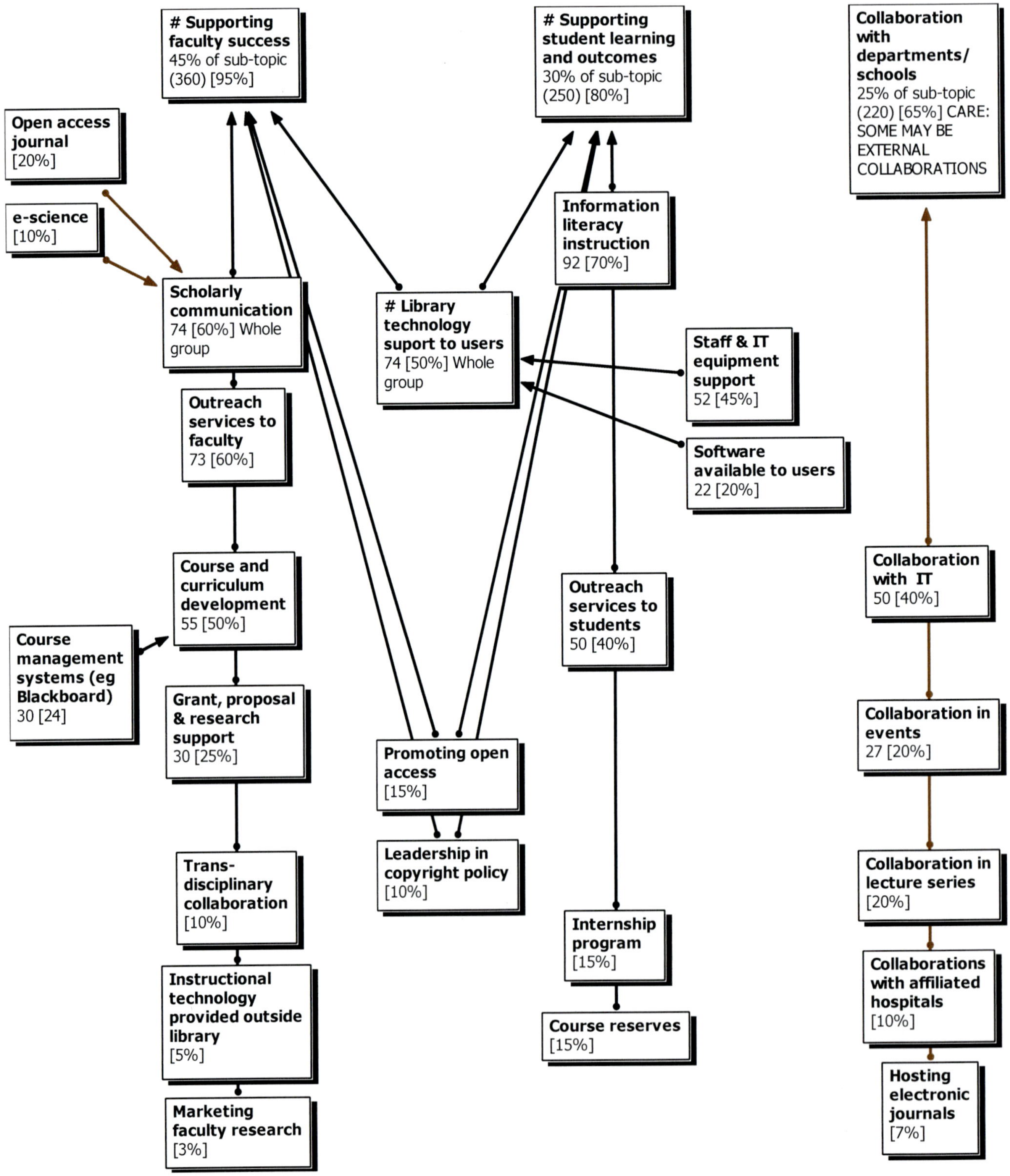

LIBRARY SERVICES – MORE FREQUENT TOPICS

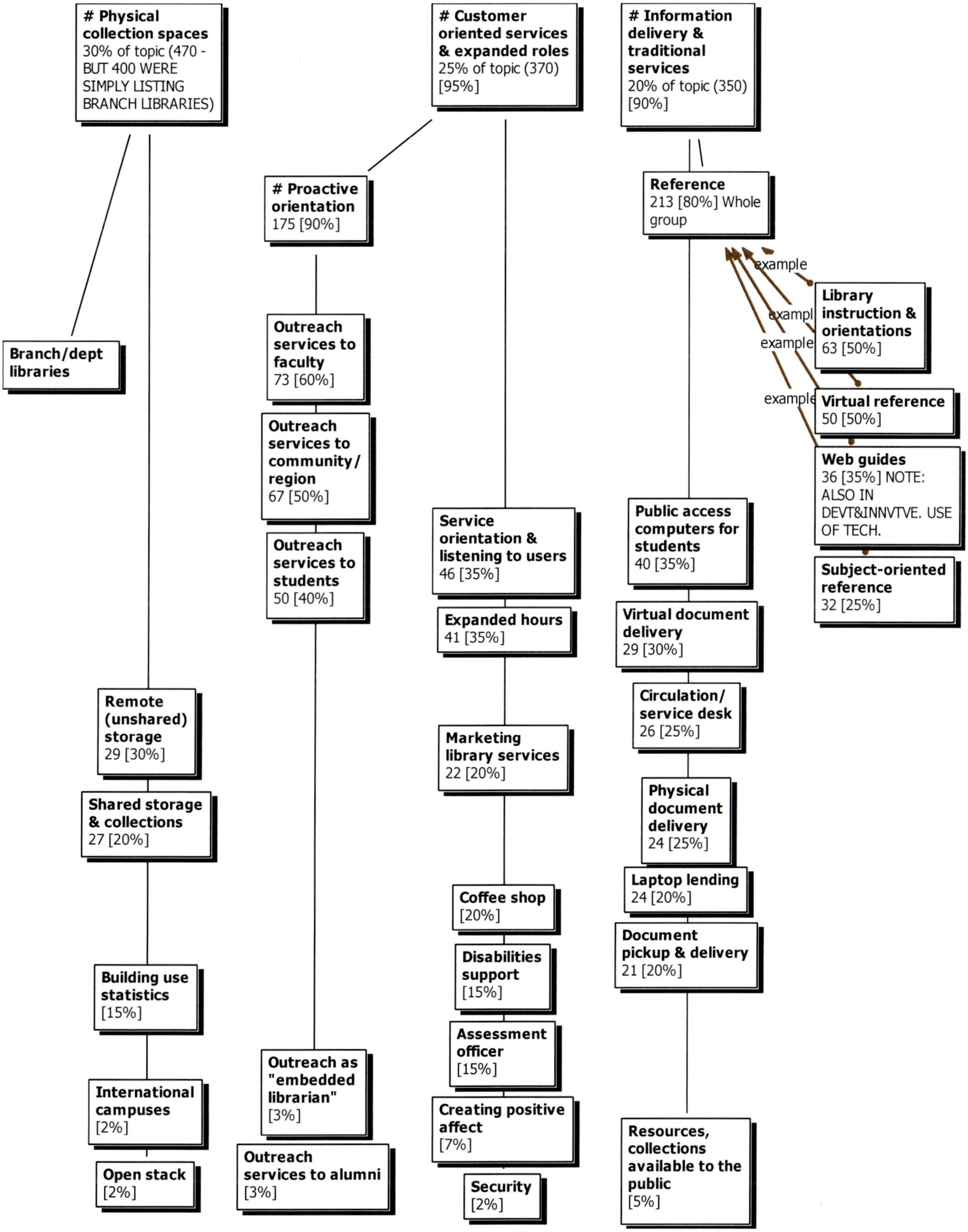

BRANCH LIBRARY DETAIL

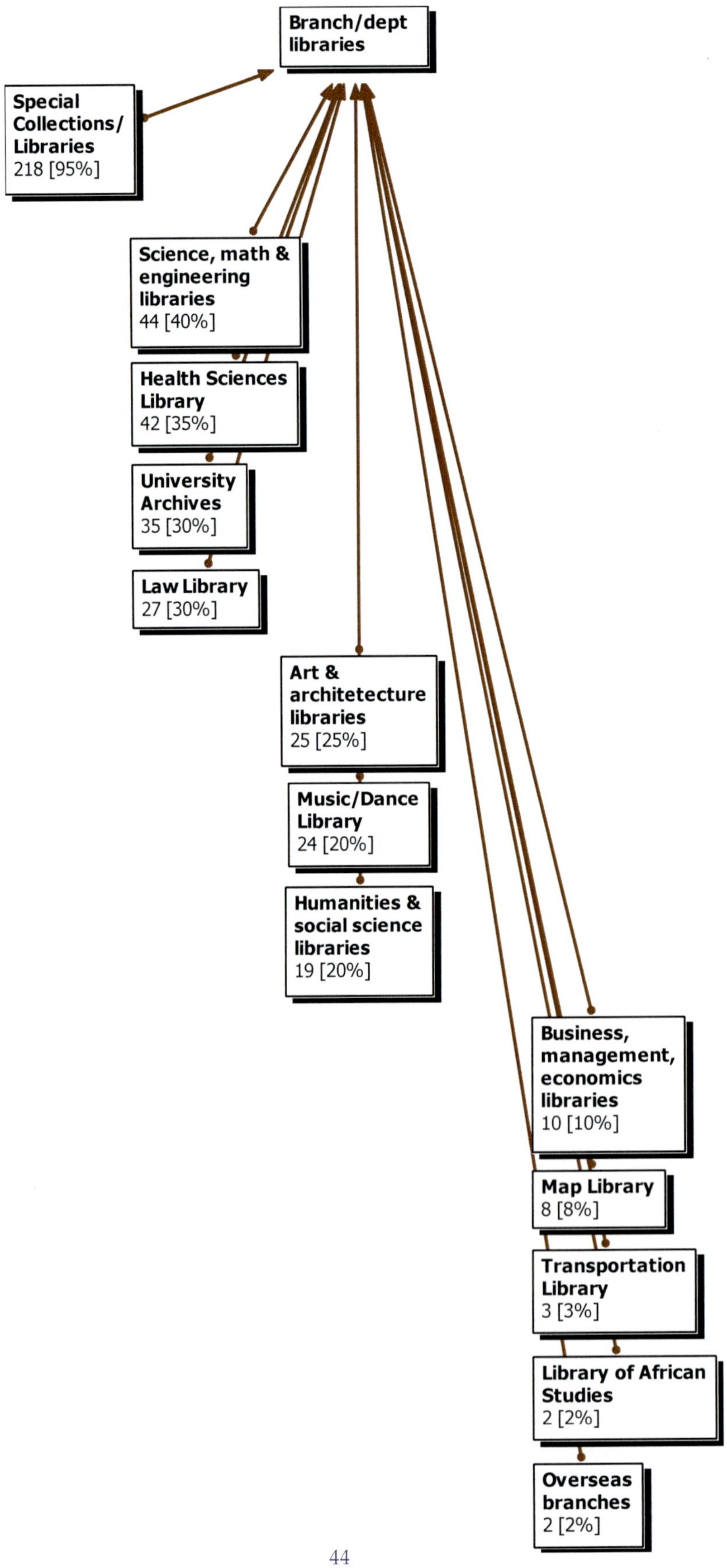

LIBRARY SERVICES – LESS FREQUENT TOPICS

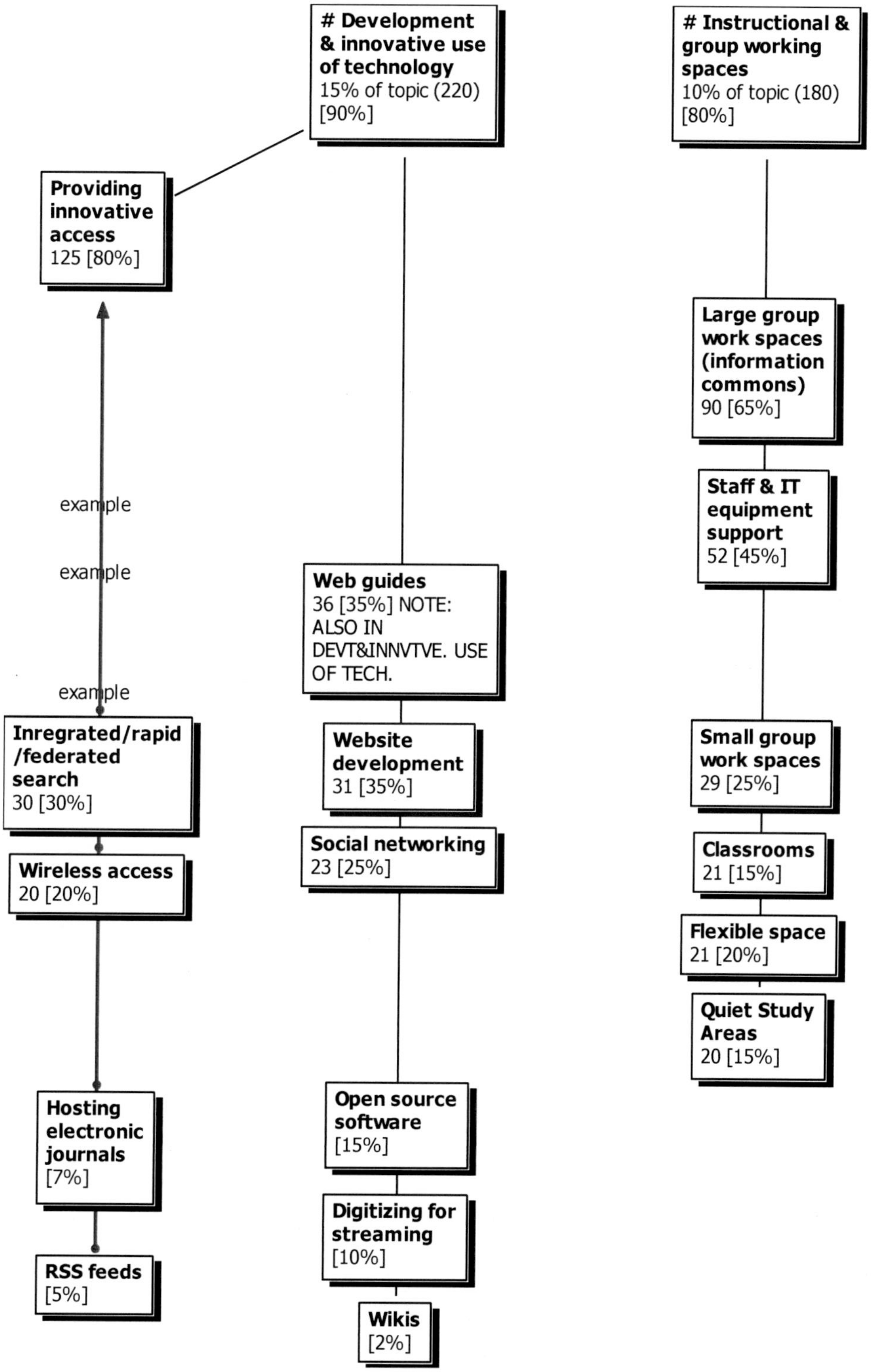

COLLECTIONS

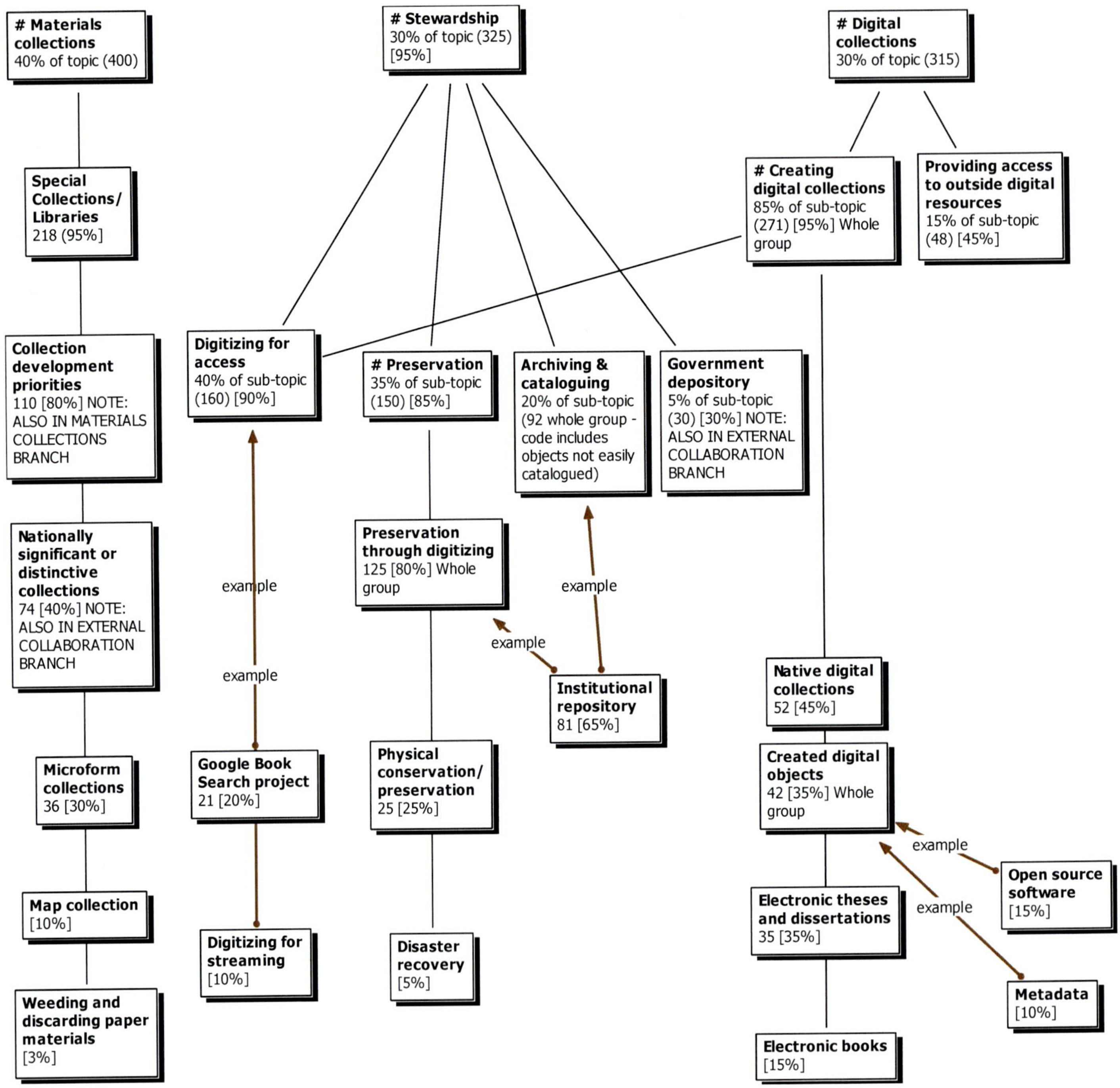

Links to Appendices

Appendix A: Content Analysis of ARL Profiles

http://www.arl.org/bm~doc/appendixa.pdf

Appendix B: ARL Profiles Invitation

http://www.arl.org/bm~doc/appendix-b.pdf

Appendix C: Profiles from ARL Members

http://www.arl.org/bm~doc/appendix-c.pdf

Technical Notes

http://www.arl.org/bm~doc/technical-notes.pdf

Digital Scholarship Quotations

http://www.arl.org/bm~doc/digital-scholarship-quotations.pdf

Frequency Explorations

http://www.arl.org/bm~doc/frequency_explorations-4th-draft.xls

Made in United States
Orlando, FL
06 November 2026

90241460R00031